THE BEST OF GOD IN MY WORST MOMENTS

Foreword by

EVANGELIST NICKY CRUZ

THE BEST OF GOD IN MY WORST MOMENTS

RAÚL QUIÑONES

RQ PUBLISHING
Colorado Springs, CO

ISBN-13: 979-8-218-08180-5

LCCN: 2022918071

TABLE OF CONTENTS

Dedication & Acknowledgments

I want to dedicate this book to God, my savior, my everything. Thanks to Him, I have a story to share of what He has done in my life through His forgiveness, mercy, and love toward me when I did not deserve it. The story of my past does not qualify me to write this book, and the testimonies that are written aren't based on my own efforts, merits, or works to change and save me because I tried many times and failed. These pages speak of what He did in my past when I was lost and aimless, and it speaks about my present in which He gives me purpose and a new reason to live.

God took this vessel of mud, the vile and despised of the world to heal, restore, save, and raise to show His love, transforming power and purpose in my life. Without Him, life has no meaning or reason, but in His hands, I found His calling for my life, the desire to live for Him, and an unforgettable experience that marked my life forever. My love and appreciation for Him is what I can offer Him since I cannot repay what He did, is still doing, and what He will do for me.

I want to thank my mother, Abad Echevarría, for being that woman of God who stood in the gap for me to intercede when I was lost in a world of darkness. Her love for me, her faith, and her commitment to God made her shed many tears in prayer, believing and knowing that, one day, God would reach her son and save him and use him for His glory and honor.

I also want to thank my family for supporting me, praying for me, and loving me in every moment and under all circumstances. Their support has been crucial during times of peace and storms and times of sadness and despair. Their love and persistence in believing in me has been the anchor that has sustained me and has given me the strength and passion to keep going without looking back.

I close with these acknowledgments with a special mention to Minister Juan Alberto Ovalle, who called me to tell me that God had shown him the title of this beautiful book you carry today.

FOREWORD

I hope you are moved to read this book, which teaches how God protected this man of God and his family to deal with all the abuse of his childhood. This book will help you and many families to have the courage to examine the situation they are going through and make the decision to seek change. It will help people struggling with depression and those who feel lonely and abandoned.

We can't deny this miracle in Raul and his family. These books tells how God took him out of the world and out of the depths of despair, insecurity, fear, hate, and self-destruction.

Raul has touched a point that many cannot understand, but God is a God of miracles because Raul is a miracle. This anointed man teaches two kinds of love: human love and divine love. When these two elements come together, something supernatural happens in a person's life.

Raul has been a personal blessing. I immediately knew when I learned the contents he would be sharing in these pages that the Spirit of the Living God would move and shake the innermost and hidden parts of our minds and hearts. It is so real that it will lead us to recognize God's grace in action and the power of the Holy Spirit transforming a life that seemed impossible to change.

The excellence of this book is that it has many elements we need to understand and help awaken in us the desire to evangelize and go out and rescue the lives that await each of us, as there much need, even in the midst of our own families.

When I think about his beginnings, his childhood, I can only think that Raul was doomed to fail from the beginning, but God rescued him. His mom practiced spiritism, so Raul was conceived under that curse. From that womb, he was birthed, and his life was destined to be lost.

If you need a reference, I invite you to read Psalm 40:1–3. There you will understand from where God rescued Raul, from that muddy lake and horrible life. He didn't have a paternal figure to cover him. And although he was surrounded by everything that could maintain him on a path toward death, God came into the life of Raul's mom, and she became one of the most powerful intercessors of her times, who provoked God's favor in the life of Raul through her prayers.

Pastor Raul joined the Army, trying to get away from the world of drugs, Santería (African diasporic religion), and wars for control of drug points; however, God took him to three different territories with a divine plan: to jail, to the desert, and to a deathbed. But God always had a plan with him. God is a God that when He changes and wants to change a person, no one can imagine how He will do it.

Raul is a wonder and a miracle. I love him as a son, he is a powerful preacher, and I have listened to his sermons and have been a witness to the lives he has earned for Christ. I have seen him overcome strong trials, one after another, without giving up along the way. I have seen him cry on many occasions and have also witnessed many miracles in his family. In his last trial in the face of death, I was also a witness to the entire process and once again saw how God saved his life. Possibly for this time, God preserved him, and today you have the opportunity through his testimony to receive an injection of faith to see the best of God in his worst moments.

Evangelist Nicky Cruz

THE BORICUA IN MACEDONIA –
THIS WASN'T A FAIRY TALE

You were not supposed to have this book in your hands. My family should have been bringing me flowers to the cemetery for years now, and I should just be a mere memory. If I were to share with you every experience in which I have seen the hand of God in my life, I would have to write an encyclopedia instead of a book, and even then, there wouldn't be enough space. This book that you have today in your hands is a dream and an assignment I have been carrying for years. I tried on many occasions to write and publish it, but for various reasons, it wasn't possible. Today I am fully aware that there were still many things I had to go through that needed to be included as testimonies of victory.

This book is a live testimony of a mother who always believed and never gave up because she was in line with what God had spoken over and for her son. Mother or father who may be reading this book, I am a product of a mother's prayer. Never give up! You possibly do not see in your children today what your heart desires, but continue believing and speaking into their spirits what God has spoken over them. It took me years to get to the place God wanted, but once I did, I have never left.

What are you going to read in this book? There are three real moments where I saw myself on the verge of death, but God was always there. You will see the hand of God work in the life of an imperfect man, but one who carried a special assignment from the Father, and until this assignment is fulfilled on earth, God will continue walking with him until this purpose is accomplished.

God didn't deliver me from jail nor punishment, but He delivered me from death. My role as a preacher and pastor did not start on the altar with a microphone, but behind bars and in a desert. My life in God has not been free of trials and tribulations, and I have had to dance with death on multiple occasions, and God has delivered me from all of them.

This is why my expectations for you is that by reading this beautiful testimony, you will realize that when God has a purpose with you, He will always be faithful in fulfilling it. The same way that He DIDN'T deliver Daniel from the lion's den but was there with him, the same way He DIDN'T deliver Job during his losses but watched over his soul, and the same way He DIDN'T prevent Joseph from going through all of his trials but watched over him and, in the end, received retribution, HE WILL DO IT WITH YOU!

Life Sentence

I was born in Brooklyn, New York, and grew up in a dysfunctional family where my dad was an alcoholic and an absent father. I don't ever recall him expressing any love toward me or telling me that he loved me. He abused my older brothers who were his stepsons, and I am not just referring to physical abuse; he also sexually abused my older sister.

When I was a kid, I remember seeing strangers come over and read the tarot cards to my dad, and they would wash his feet afterward. In my house, they practiced witchcraft, and there were diabolic manifestations that my older brothers were able to witness. I didn't understand what was going on. One of the events I remember was when my dad was possessed one day, and he took a knife and wanted to kill the whole family. My older brother got up and closed the door to avoid my dad getting out of the room. My brother Eddie was holding the door, and my dad was stabbing through it while my brother was yelling at us to run. The whole family ran into the backyard while my brother held the door, allowing us to escape and save our lives. He stood there as long as he could and then ran out.

This incident caused my brother to speak to a friend to get him a gun to kill my dad. My mom, who was already serving the Lord, told her pastor my brother's plan and he decided to collect an offering so that we could get out of the circumstances in which we found ourselves. We left New York and came to Puerto Rico and stayed for some time with my older brothers' aunt.

Afterward, a person from the church helped us, and we were able to rent a small room in an apartment. We didn't have anything because we had fled New York from the situation our father had put us in.

Some years passed, and I was eight years old when my mom gave us the news that my dad had died. I later found out that he had committed suicide. From that moment, my life became impacted by the absence of a father in my life.

Many times, our society ignores the role of leadership and the importance of a father in the family. We ignore the influence that it provides to the whole family. We see how in the garden of Eden, Eve took the fruit that God had forbidden them to eat, and sin immediately entered them, and as soon as they realized they were naked, they went to hide. God, when finding them, spoke directly to Adam to confront him with the bad decision they had made (Gen. 6:3–12). God had established the man to lead by example in words and actions. His role was designed to impact the family.

I loved sports, so I started playing basketball and participated in boxing and baseball. When I was playing baseball, I would see that when my friends were at bat, their fathers would scream and cheer them on from the sides, but when it was my turn at bat, I would stand firm on the plate to look at the pitch. I also looked out at the benches, also hoping for my father's support and encouragement, but I only saw his absence, and this caused pain in my heart. I missed having a father tell me, "Raul I am here for you. Hit the ball hard; I know you can do it!"

Thankfully, I had a mother who served the Lord with all her heart and prayed for her family. We weren't rich, and we lacked some of the basic materialistic things, but we had the Word of God and a mother who served as an example and testimony of what it was like to serve the Lord. As a child, she took us to church, and not going wasn't an option. As soon as we arrived, she would warn us on how our behavior should be in the house of God. I grew up watching my mom pray, persevering in church, and being an example of what she taught us.

The absence of my father was always present in my heart when I was young, and it affected my development and identity. I got involved with some friends from where I lived, and I started to experiment with the world of drugs and walking around with guns.

The mother who raised a Christian boy was now witnessing her son take the opposite direction to how she raised us, but I remember that my mom always told us that salvation was an individual choice, and I would always tell her, "No Mom, when the Lord comes to take you, I am going to hold on to your skirt and go with you." She would tell me that it would not occur like that because the Lord would come in a blink of an eye (1 Cor. 15:52). Mi mom told me: "I have raised you in the ways of the Lord and have taught you the principles of the Word of God, but now that you are an adult, you have to make your own decisions."

I became involved in drug trafficking and drug sales. I sank deeper into this way of life each time, and as time went by, my mom no longer recognized me as that child raised in the gospel and with good grades in school. However, my mom trusted the Word of God in Proverbs 22:6, "Direct your children onto the right path, and when they are older, they will not leave it." My mother was a woman of faith who lived a life on her knees in prayer and was not going to let that what her natural eyes saw get in the way of her confidence in the power of God to bring her son back, just as the story of the prodigal son in the book of Luke 15:11–32.

I began with a small group that started growing in power, money, and influence in the world of drugs in our city of Bayamon, Puerto Rico. There was something I was carrying in my heart against my father, and it was because he wasn't there while I was growing up, I held a grudge and hatred for him, and I said, "I am going to punish you for being absent in my life, and now I will shame you." Even though my dad had committed suicide and was already dead, I felt I had the capacity to hurt him by doing bad things and punish him for being absent in my life.

This life I lived also introduced me to Santería. I started thinking that God couldn't help me in this world I lived in, so I thought that some opposing force would have to help me. I remember one time I went to visit the Santería priest (*santero*) for a session, and he told me to bring him a live white dove and a coconut with water inside. During the session, he told me to bend over, and he split the coconut and spilled the water over my head. Then he took the dove and passed it all over my body, from head to toe. Suddenly, he killed the dove and placed it in a bag for me so that I could throw it in a cemetery because, according to him, I had been cleansed. I was not aware of what the Bible said: "But if we confess our sins to him, he is faithful and just to forgive us our sins and to cleanse us from all wickedness." (1 John 1:9).

In the world that I was living in, I didn't realize that I was walking blindly, with no sense of where I was going. Santería provided a means for me to feel secure and have some type of protection, when, in reality, I was bringing in the world of darkness and Satan's inferno. I couldn't understand that, without God, I am nothing or can achieve anything. The *santero* gave me a necklace with seven colors and when I wore it, it crossed my body from one side to the other, and a penny at the end connected and closed the necklace. He said that each color represented a saint who gave me power and protected me. He also gave me a smooth black stone and told me that the black stone was made in Haiti. He told me that every time I saw the police (because he knew that I was in the drug world), to keep the stone in my pocket, and when the police came, I only had to squeeze it, and they would go away. He was practically giving me the impression that I would be untouchable with the police as long as I kept this stone in my pocket. For a person like me in this underground world, this was an ideal stone.

I remember I was in the projects with guys on one occasion, and the police busted in. All the guys started to run, but I stayed where I was because I had the stone in my pocket, and once I was I squeezed it, nothing would happen to me. So, I reached inside my pocket and squeezed the stone. A police officer grabbed me by the shirt, put me against the wall, and told me to put my hands against the wall. I said to myself, "This piece of junk stone seems to be out of battery because it didn't work." I believe God was teaching me that what I was putting my trust in had no power and was only a deceitful act from Satan to try to convince me that I was doing the right thing. God was allowing me to see the limitations that the enemy had and that true power came from Him, but I was blind to what had just happened and decided not to remove the necklace.

One day I got home, took my shirt off, and placed the necklace on top of it on my dresser, and my mother, who is a Christian woman raised in a Pentecostal church and had been serving the Lord for a long time, saw the necklace and asked me what type of necklace that was, and I told her that it had been prepared by a *santero* and that if she touched it, she would faint because it had power. As soon as I said that, she immediately took the necklace in her hands, looked me in the eyes, and said, "In the name of Jesus, this junk does not have the power to hurt me," and she threw it on the floor. I was shocked because the effects I thought would happen did not occur but that she remained firm, trusting in the God that she served. This made me doubt the views I had about the world of Santería. Nevertheless, I didn't stop using the necklace. God was trying to show me, although I couldn't perceive it at that moment, His desire to open my eyes to the dark world in which I found myself.

I continued in the world of drugs, and as often happens, there were rival groups with their own territories that were at odds with those who were just starting out. This always brings debate or war for the power of drug control and produces wars between rival groups.

I remember one day not going to a place where some of the group would normally get together to drink alcohol. That day a car pulled up with different armed individuals, and they began shooting inside the premises. Several people were injured, and two crew members were killed. One never expects these things can happen, but in the world where we found ourselves, it was part of our norm. The deaths within our group began for the first time, and this sparked a war against the other rival group.

As payback for what they had done, we decided to visit the projects from where these enemies came. We had planned to surround the projects, and two of my friends and I would go straight to a specific apartment to execute those people. When we arrived as planned, we went to the apartment and kicked in the door, but the people who were supposed to be there weren't. We ran from one side to the other inside the apartment, looking for our enemies to avenge the death of our friends, but we didn't find them. We had to leave without results. I could firmly understand that the hand of God was with me to prevent me from falling into an even deeper situation in the world where I found myself. Well, I had a mother who continued to pray and intercede for me so that God would rescue me from the place I was in.

After that incident, we were attacked in our projects, and they caught me off guard at that moment. Our enemies entered the place we were at the same moment I was outside walking with a friend. Suddenly I heard a woman scream my name from a balcony, and when I turned around to look at the person who was calling me, I saw a man dressed in black, holding what appeared to be a rifle at a distance of fifteen to twenty feet away from me. As soon as I turned around, he opened fire at us. I turned around and pushed my friend and told him to start running, and then I started running. It was as if time had stopped when the person behind me began to shoot. I had enough time to turn around to see him, turn back around to push my friend, and start running before he started shooting. It was impossible for him to miss since he was so close and in position.

While he was shooting at me, I saw the bullets hit the wall next to me as I ran, trying to go up to an apartment. As I went up the stairs of this apartment, I could feel the bullets hitting the sole of my shoes, but they didn't touch my feet or body. I started to knock on a door, and when they opened the door, I forced myself inside to protect myself from the shooter since I thought he was still behind me. So I dropped to the floor of the apartment and took out the gun I carried on my waist and aimed toward the door, waiting for him to appear, but that never happened; they had already left the place.

God continued to answer my mother's prayers since death came very close to me, but God continued to protect me. God used a woman on a balcony to warn me of the eminent danger that was behind me that I had not even noticed. Once I realized they had left the projects, I left the apartment to go look for my friend. I saw every bullet hole along the way where I had run, and none of these bullets had touched me or done me harm.

It seemed like God had paused time during this event to give me the opportunity to look back after hearing the woman on the balcony, turn around, yell at my friend to run, push him along, and run for safety as well. This all happened while this person was already behind me, long before the woman on the balcony could shout to warn me. To this day, I keep in mind that the shooter must have been in disbelief as to how it was possible that I could get out of that event unscathed. He was in a very easy position to kill me, and as he shot straight at me, the bullets deflected and hit the wall. I remember that when I got home that night, my girlfriend, who is now my wife, told me she was at home with my mom when the first shots were heard because we lived near where the shooting took place. She said my mother immediately knew those bullets were directed at her son without her knowing I was involved.

My little brother began having nightmares where he saw me inside a casket and would frequently find my mom crying desperately because of the situation I was in. While trying to help me, my mom would ask the brothers and sisters of the church to come to the house and do prayer services so that they could pray and intercede for me. Sometimes I would come home and see them singing Christian songs, and my mom would detain me so that they could pray for me, which I was just not interested in because I was blind to the world in which I found myself.

My mother did everything in her power so that God could reach my life and change it. But we know God is not a God who comes early or late but just in time and that my mother's prayer had come before God. It was a matter of time before my dark days would come to an end, and I would be willing to hear His voice. The Word of God tells us in Jeremiah 33:3, "Ask me and I will tell you remarkable secrets you do not know about things to come." This verse had become real for my mother and would soon be real in my life as well.

After that incident where I was almost killed, the rival group came back to attack us, and this time, they killed other friends of our group. The situation had become very serious to the point that my family could no longer deal with the danger in which I found myself. They advised and convinced me to go for a while with my brother-in-law to the state of Mississippi in the United States. And that is what I did. It was very hard to adapt at first. I had nobody from back home close to me nor the places where I used to hang out. I had to adapt to this new place.

Even though I left the drug world and Santería behind in Puerto Rico, I was still living a lifestyle that wasn't beneficial to me. The life of a person doesn't just change because we move from one place, but it is transformed when we surrender our lives at the feet of Christ and accept him as the Lord and Savior of our lives. It is then when change truly begins in our lives, from the inside out.

After spending time with my brother-in-law, he received orders to report to Japan because he was in the military. I found myself with nowhere to go because returning to Puerto Rico was not an option for the moment, and staying by myself in the US wasn't an option either. So, I decided to enlist in the US Armed Forces.

The first unit they sent me off to was in Germany. After spending a few months there, we received a mission to be part of the United Nations. We needed to report to Macedonia, a province in what was Yugoslavia because there had been a war where genocide was taking place, and we were there to stop the war that was already taking place.

After serving there for several months, I was keeping guard in front of several buildings where the different countries under the United Nations met. Suddenly my sergeant major told me that the colonel wished to speak with me, so he asked me to give my rifle to my sergeant, and then he would return me to my post. This whole time I had no idea what was happening, but when I heard my sergeant major say that the colonel wished to speak to me, and since I was a new soldier, I thought that they were that they were going to raise me in rank, but it wasn't typical for the colonel to do these ceremonies.

I arrived before him, escorted by my sergeant major and the military police. I stood at attention, gave him the military salute, and waited for his instructions. He started speaking to me and telling me I was a good soldier, but those positive words were followed by: "You have the right to remain silent. Anything you say can and will be used against you in a court of law. You have a right to an attorney. If you can't afford an attorney, one will be appointed to you by the State." I realized they were reading me my rights, and the military police was arresting me.

My whole body started to shake, and my knees kept knocking on each other because I could not understand what was happening. One minute they told me I was a good soldier, and the next, they arrested me. He told the officer to cuff me at the hands and feet. The colonel then proceeded to tell me that I was a fugitive of the law and that the federal police had a warrant for my arrest for several murders. I walked out of his office with my hands and feet cuffed, walking toward a military airplane while all the soldiers were shocked to see me in chains walking past them.

The reason why my sergeant major had not told me what the meeting with the colonel was about was because I had a rifle in my hands, and with the information he had received in advance, he thought I was dangerous and could react violently. That day it seemed like the whole world came down on me and that now my life was taking a turn toward a place I thought would never end. It felt like a dark cloud had settled over me. I began to think that I had joined the Army to change my life, but now my past was catching up with me and was able to reach me at the most unexpected time and place.

After boarding the plane, they took me to Germany where they would later transfer me to the United States and finally to Puerto Rico, where charges had been filed against me and where there was an arrest and extradition warrant to face the charges against me.

Once I arrived in Germany, they kept me in a military jail while I awaited extradition to the United States arrived. While there, they assigned two soldiers to guard my cell for twenty-four hours. I remember that if I went to use the bathroom, I had to be accompanied by the two armed soldiers, and in the same way, if I wanted to brush my teeth, one of them would hold his gun while the other would open the cell to carefully place the toothpaste and toothbrush in my hands and then close the cell. Apart from the armed soldiers, the cell had a camera recording me at all times. A letter written by the United States Department of the Army stated I was very dangerous, so they tried to be vigilant in everything they did.

During all of this time, I never knew that I was a fugitive from justice back home in Puerto Rico and that there were serious accusations against me. Then the moment arrived where they were going to extradite me from this temporary jail in Germany to the United States of America. I would be escorted by a military soldier who would deliver me to the federal police once I arrived at the airport in the United States. That soldier was a muscular African American, standing at around six feet four inches.

On our way toward the airport, the soldier told me that, by law, he could not cuff my hands and feet because it was a long flight. So, he gave me a warning that if I tried to run, it wasn't going to be a pretty sight. While he was warning me, I kept looking at his muscles and his height, and at no time did the desire to try to run from him cross my mind. So, wherever he moved, I moved with him, no questions asked.

After many hours, we finally arrived in the United States to Philadelphia. When the plane landed, I heard the pilot tell the crew to remain in their seats because there was a passenger that needed to deboard first, and that was me. When I looked out the window, I saw the plane surrounded by cops. Anyone would say that the president of the United States was on this plane with so many police and protection outside.

As soon as the flight attendant opened the door for me to get out, the federal police immediately told the US Army soldier that they had full custody of me, so they put my hands against the wall and chained my hands and feet. I never thought I would feel so ashamed to be chained up like an animal all over the airport.

They immediately put me in a vehicle that would take me to a jail in Philadelphia while I waited for the Puerto Rican police officers to come and extradite me. Once I arrived at the jail, they placed me in a cold and empty cell. When they closed the gate of the cell, it was then that reality hit me in the face, and I realized everything that had happened up to that moment. This wasn't a dream or nightmare; my life had taken a turn, and I had no idea where I was headed.

Something unexpected happened while I was locked up in there for twenty-four hours a day. Suddenly I started feeling a presence that filled the cell, but I couldn't see anything; I just felt that it was invaded by something supernatural. At that moment, I realized that this supernatural presence was nothing more and nothing less than the presence of Jesus that came at the most difficult moment of my life and where my mind was totally confused by what was happening.

Tears began to flow down my cheeks at that moment, and I knew that Jesus was visiting me. I proceeded to speak aloud with that presence that was real and powerful all at once. I told Jesus that I knew He was there and that I didn't understand why He was there after having turned my back on Him for so long. So, I confessed to Jesus everything that I had experienced everything the world had offered me. I acknowledged up to what point this world I was living at had brought me, but if He had something better than what I had experienced, I was willing to open my heart to Him as Lord and Savior of my life so that I could experience something new.

At no time was I giving my heart to Jesus to deliver me from that place, but I realized that everything I had done in my life had fallen apart and had no value. I felt the need to experience something new that could fill the void in my heart, and that was the moment when I gave Jesus the opportunity to show me something new and transformative that could change my life. That day started off toward something powerful that I didn't understand, but I knew it was better than anything I had experienced in the past. There began something new and different, where I gave the helm of my life to Jesus so that now He would guide me to a safe harbor.

After being at the Philadelphia jail for a period of time, two federal police officers (marshals) finally arrived to extradite me to the island of Puerto Rico to face the charges against me. Once again, they cuffed my hands and feet, and I had to walk through all the people at the airport, and this time, my flight was a commercial flight, where everyone could see there was a dangerous person onboard.

When the food was served on the plane, I asked the federal police to release the handcuffs so I could eat, to which they said that would not be possible, so with handcuffed hands, I had to eat my dinner, doing my best to get the food to my mouth. I don't know if they thought that at 34,000 feet in the air, I was going to escape. They were treating me to that extent because they thought I was extremely dangerous.

When the plane finally landed at the airport in Puerto Rico, I saw the same situation that had happened to me when I had arrived in Philadelphia. When I looked out the window, there were many police officers surrounding the plane, and when I stepped out before anyone else, the local police were already waiting for me.

As the police escorted me into a police vehicle, they were intercepted by several news reporters who asked me if I was innocent or guilty of the charges against me.

Before I was extradited to Puerto Rico, my mother had a dream that she saw me cuffed at both hands and feet, and she had told one of her sisters at church. She described how she had seen me, but this sister said it was impossible since I was an active soldier in the Army. In addition to the dream, God had instructed my mother to fast for ten days with just vegetables because the last thing she would expect was to see her son extradited to Puerto Rico in handcuffs. It was the way her spirit was preparing her for what was to come.

Several days had passed when my mother was watching television, and a last-minute news bulletin appeared, announcing that Raul Quiñones had been arrested, and they nicknamed me "the man from Macedonia" because I had been arrested during in a mission in that province that was former Yugoslavia. It was that moment when my mother saw the son she had raised in the gospel, cuffed at the hands and feet. God had prepared her beforehand with the dream and the fast, which gave her the strength she needed when she saw me through her television screen.

They took me before a judge who set a seven-million-dollar bail for the four murder charges, attempted murder, and twenty-one counts of weapons charges. If found guilty, I would face 305 years in jail.

Since I wasn't able to pay the bail, I was incarcerated in a local jail called "El Oso Blanco" in Rio Piedras, Puerto Rico. In that jail, there were about seven or eight other inmates in the section where I was, called the "Intensive Treatment Unit."

The cells were open at all times, and inside the jail, there was, and still is, an organization called "La Asociación Ñeta" (The Ñeta Association), which have their own rules to maintain respect and coexistence among the inmates.

When I got to my section, the guard asked me if I was a member of the Ñetas or part of another group that also existed in the jail, with which I had no experience to know which group I belonged. So, he asked me about the charges against me, and he immediately told me I needed to be with the Ñetas.

Once in the section, one of the inmates told me my cell was the last one at the end of the corridor. While heading toward my cell, I noticed another inmate had several blades in his hands—the kind that are made in a jail—and was sharpening them to put them away later. During the first few days, I couldn't sleep because I kept wondering that if one of the enemies I had made in the streets was in there with me, this would be his opportunity to end my life. So, I would get up late at night, making sure that all the inmates were sleeping before I went to rest. To my surprise, by the grace of God that was now upon me as His son, I was in favor with all of them.

The inmates with me began to respect me because they knew I was a Christian, and my actions were a reflection that God had changed my life. I shared with them the accusations against me, and I remember we were gathered in a circle, and they understood my innocence against all of the accusations against me. It was interesting when I finished sharing my legal situation because others started to say they were also innocent and that their cases were fabricated. One of the inmates sarcastically and jokingly told the others, "I believe Raul is innocent, but now all of you want to play the innocent victim when we all know we are here because of the things we did. You hear his story, and now you want to make yourselves innocent." The rest began to laugh, but he was sure to state that he knew my case was different from the rest.

Preachers from the community would frequently come to the institution to preach and pray, and one day an evangelist came to minister the Word of God. After he delivered his sermon, he asked us to grab hands and pray together. While he was praying, I felt something enter through my head as if it were a lightning bolt, and it penetrated me to the point where I felt something break off of me. At that moment, I started to shout words of adoration and praise to God at the top of my lungs. I didn't understand why I was reacting that way. I later understood that God had baptized me with his Holy Spirit and fire and was preparing me for a special assignment that I did not fully understand.

When I started to worship God aloud, the other inmates started to look at me. I felt I was walking through the clouds when a supernatural peace overtook me. I started to prophesy over the lives of the other inmates without knowing what that was, and I said to them that they needed to surrender their lives to the Lord. They started to cry because they were reacting to the voice of God. I didn't know what it meant to prophesy, and I didn't understand what I was telling them on God's behalf, but it was as if the Holy Spirit took my mouth under His command to deliver a message.

That night, the presence of God was so strong and tangible that we were able to feel how He was moving among us. It's incredible how the presence of the Holy Spirit can come into a dark place to bring light to the lives of those who have committed crimes. This is why the Word of God states in John 3:16, "For God so loved the world that He gave His only Son. Whoever puts his trust in God's Son will not be lost but will have life that lasts forever. For God did not send His Son into the world to say it is guilty. He sent His Son so the world might be saved from the punishment of sin by Him."

That day when the service was over in the chapel, I immediately went back to my cell and went on my knees. I told God I wanted Him to use me how He used the evangelist Yiye Ávila. I was obviously ignorant of what I was asking for, but I remember when I was five years old, I saw this man at Madison Square Garden in New York, of whom my mother had spoken to me . I asked my mom if he could heal me because I suffered from nosebleeds, and every time I went to sleep, I would wake up with a pillow full of blood. Since I saw people being healed at the campaign, that was the reason I was asking. My mom explained to me that he couldn't heal me but that God could use this man when he prayed over me to do it. We have to take into account that we are an influence for better or worse, depending on the decisions we make. This man of God had a huge impact in my life, so much so that years later, I still remember his ministry.

In that section of the prison where I was assigned, I started to become a positive influence on my companions, not only with words but with the testimony of what God was doing in my life. After being there for a certain time, the penal system decided to move me to a more restrictive cell due to the charges I was facing. So, they put me in a maximum-security prison called "El Monstruo Verde" (the green monster), where I would be locked up for twenty-three hours a day, seven days a week, and they only took me out for an hour a week. The jail had that name because it was surrounded by green mountains and was highly secured.

That move from a minimum-security jail to maximum security took a huge toll on me. It took me to a condition where I questioned my relationship with God. I continued to ask myself how God could allow me to end up in a worse place than I was. But God, who knows all the plans and purposes He has for His children, knows what is best for us. God works with plans that are aligned with what He has designed for our lives. What we have to do is trust Him and allow His sovereignty and power to fulfill His plans in our lives.

At this new place, they had me share a cell with an inmate who was missing an eye and was addicted to drugs. This inmate barely received visitors, but that's where I was assigned. I noticed this inmate did not have the twelve-inch television that the inmates were allowed to have, and he didn't have any other means of communication, such as a radio, to entertain himself. The cell had a shower inside and everything necessary so that we didn't have to leave that small place. I tried to request a cell change with another inmate who at least had a TV so that I could keep myself entertained, but it was denied.

My mother had sent me a small radio and a Bible that I started to read as if it were any other book since I didn't have much knowledge regarding the Word of God. I also began to listen to sermons and the Christian station that transmitted through the radio. I told my cellmate that I was a Christian, so we shared the small radio and listened to the sermons together every night. Since I didn't have much to do, I read the whole Bible and told my cellmate I had finished reading it. He told me the Bible was a never-ending book, so he insisted I read it again, even though he wasn't a Christian. God was using him to motivate me to grow in my relationship with God was growing and, at the same time, be a witness to him.

One day when the patrolling guard passing by, guided by the Holy Spirit, I took a risk and stopped him so that we could speak. I asked if there was a possibility that I could come out of the cell to preach to the other inmates, something that had never been done in that place. I told him I was a Christian, and he looked at me doubtfully as if to say, "Of course, you're a Christian. That's why you are here." But when God is involved in our matters, there is nothing that could stop His plans, so during that conversation, he said he would approve my request and that I could preach after the last meal of the day.

Even so, there was another obstacle, the organization inside the prison called "La Asociación Ñeta" that lived by their own rules, as I had mentioned before. I needed to speak with the person in charge of my section so that he could give me the final approval. I was on the third floor of the penitentiary, but the leader was located on the first floor, so I had to yell my intentions to him to preach to the rest of the inmates. He started telling all of the inmates to come forward to their cell doors to listen to my proposal to preach to them inside the jail. Surprisingly, all the inmates started to yell from their cells that they supported the idea. My heart was so full of joy that there were no words to describe what I was feeling.

I remembered the Evangelist Yiye Ávila, whom my mother spoke to me about as an example to follow. I learned that he fasted and prayed before every campaign so that God would back him up during his preaching events. It was difficult to fast inside this jail because I received little food, but I knew that it was vital to fast, pray, and study the Word of God. So, I turned to the Lord in prayer to help me through this whole process. What the prison guard and the inmates didn't know was that I had an encounter with God in that place where I had been saved and had begun to be transformed by the power of the Holy Spirit.

That impulse I felt to preach did not come from my own desires or emotions but from the Holy Spirit, who was motivating me and driving me to fulfill the purpose for which I was in that place. God was placing His will and desire by the goodness of His will in my life, so I was being guided by His Spirit. We must acknowledge that when God is in the business of opening doors to use you, nothing or no one can stop the hand of God from moving in and through our lives. Not only did God save me at that place, but He also wanted to use me as an instrument in His hands so that others could enjoy the freedom that I had found in Jesus Christ.

My third and final obstacle with preaching was that I didn't know how to preach, but I was reminded of my Sunday school teacher who taught me Bible stories as a child. One of those stories was about David and Goliath. When the day came to come out and preach, all the inmates stood in front of their cell bars, and the police officer placed me in a spot where all the inmates were able to see me from every floor. I was very nervous, but at the same time I could feel the courage that the Holy Ghost gave me. I remembered that as a child, the services began with various hymns, so I decided to start the same way. I asked the inmates to accompany me in a hymn called "Yo Tengo Un Gozo En Mi Alma" ("I've Got a Joy Like a River"). I thought the inmates would sing along, but they were all just staring at me, and after a while, I finished singing and started to preach.

My message was as short as my experience as a preacher, but I was brave enough to do it, and that brought me joy. I proceeded to do a calling since I had also learned as a kid in church when my mom use to take me, and that day no one replied to God's calling, but I did not feel discouraged. Sometimes we do things for God and immediately think we are going to see results when, in truth, God works according to His time and will, and we simply have to do the work that He commissioned us to do and leave the results to Him.

A week had gone by when I asked the guard once again if I could preach. The second time I preached, it was practically the same scenario, but I felt more confident and in control, and I could feel that something was happening in the atmosphere. On the third occasion, something unexpected occurred because when I started the service with a hymn, the inmates started to sing along; they raised their hands and jumped in their cells. Even the prison guard watching over us asked if he could listen to the message, to which I affirmed since he was the person in charge. He must have seen something different in the atmosphere to have spoken to me with those words.

After we sang, I started to preach, but this time I was attentive to what God wanted me to say and simply repeated, and the sermon kept extending. I didn't understand what was happening because I was preaching as if I had previous experience. I knew it was the direction of the Holy Spirit guiding me at all times.

At the end of the message, I made the calling and let them know that there were probably people who had forgotten about them, and that society possibly viewed them as a problem for the community; however, I let them know that there was one called Jesus who, no matter what they had done, was willing to forgive and save them if they surrendered to Him. To my surprise, the inmates started to reach out from their cells, shouting and crying that they wanted to accept Jesus. That place had been filled with God's glory and power, and lives were being impacted by His presence. Supernatural began occurring that I didn't understand, but I knew God was moving in that place.

On one occasion, the inmate association was going to punish another inmate because he had gone against the rules of the jail, and before he went to get judged, he stopped in front of my cell and asked me to pray for him. I was on the third floor when I suddenly began hearing the beatings that he was receiving from the other inmates for breaking the jail rules. When the punishment finished, he stopped once again in front of my cell and confessed that while they were beating him, he felt no pain. I knew God had answered my prayer and my faith placed in Him.

Eventually, my trial for the murder and gun charges against me began. On the way to court for one of the sessions, I noticed that I was being escorted by police cars in front, behind, and a helicopter all the way from the jail to the courthouse. I didn't understand the need for so much security until I found out who was the other inmate in the car. This person was well known in the underworld as a hitman and was being extradited from Colombia to Puerto Rico. While in the car, I heard the voice of God tell me to minister to him about salvation. I introduced myself, and he asked me why I was in jail. When I shared my charges, he stated that his were worse because he was being charged with several murders and was being extradited. That didn't stop me from talking to him about Jesus without fear of who I was talking to.

While we were being transported, I continued to speak about Jesus, and to my surprise, he was willing to accept Jesus as Lord and Savior of his life. I was experiencing things I could simply not explain, but I was being used as an instrument in the hand of God so that I could tell everyone who came in contact with me about the love of Jesus.

Later in a court holding cell while waiting to see a judge, I came across a young man who had murdered his sister because he heard a voice tell him to kill her while under the influence of drugs. I was able to recognize him because one of the inmates waiting with me recognized him from the local news that covered his case. His face seemed sad, his eyes dull and lost.

Once again, I heard the voice of God telling me to speak to him about the love of Jesus, so I approached him, introduced myself, and began evangelizing the message of salvation. When I asked if he wanted to accept Jesus as Lord and Savior, he confirmed that he wanted to accept Him and the salvation Jesus offered. In those moments when I heard the voice of God that compelled me to speak to the inmates, I also felt courage and compassion that I could not explain. The Holy

Spirit gave me the ability to minister based on their needs.

Time passed as the prosecutor continued to look for information against me while my lawyers looked for evidence of my innocence. I would appear in court and sometimes they would postpone the hearing because the prosecution's witness was not prepared to testify. Meanwhile, months passed, but God continued to sustain me throughout all this time and use me to preach His Word.

Often, we see time pass and wonder why our issues don't seem to get resolved, but God is a God who works with purpose and not with human time but according to His divine and perfect will. Although I was still waiting for my case to be heard, I knew I wasn't wasting my time but that the Lord was working in me and through me to fulfill His plans.

On another occasion, I was headed to the courthouse in a prisoner transport bus with other inmates headed to the courthouse in Bayamón, Puerto Rico, with pending cases. Suddenly, I saw that one of them took out a key to open the cuffs on his hands and feet, and he passed the key along so that the other inmates could free themselves. The guards driving the bus could not see what was happening in the back of the bus. One of the inmates asked me if I was willing to escape with them because they were waiting for the opportunity so that when the bus door opened, they could attack the guards and escape. One of them had written a letter to people on the outside who were supposed to intercept the bus so that they could escape. I told them I couldn't escape with them because I was innocent of my charges, but I was also worried of what they would do to me if they attacked the guards and I decided to stay behind. I also wondered what would happen if they had harmed the prison guards and then the police would come and find me alone on the bus with injured cops beside me.

I was in a great dilemma, not knowing what to do, but I started to pray in my mind, asking God not to allow the plans of these inmates to prosper since my life was at risk if they carried out their plans. Not even ten minutes had passed when I had finished my prayer when they began to close the cuffs of their hands and feet and changed the conversation. That was extremely impactful for me how God upset up their plans to preserve the purpose He had for me.

After several months of incarceration, the time finally had come for the prosecutors to present the evidence they had against me and for my lawyers to present my innocence. Every time I went to the court for a hearing, the room was filled with people, including news reporters. They continually interviewed me for my response to the charges against me. I always said I was innocent, and God was in control of everything that was happening.

It was very difficult and painful to see my mother, my girlfriend at the time, who is now my wife, and my daughter visit me in a place so sad and solitary. When my mother went to see me in jail, she would try to hold back her tears so that I wouldn't worry, but I was aware of her suffering. My mom always kept me in her prayers, and she is a woman of faith who trusted in God with all her heart. When she visited me, I always gave her testimony of what God was doing in me and through me.

The prosecution presented its only witness who said I was present at the scene of the crime when the murders took place and that I was one of the gang leaders, which is why he could identify me. The witness said I was the person who killed his brother at the scene of the crime. This same witness was the person responsible for placing several of our crew members under life imprisonment with his testimony, and the last one left to accuse was me.

What the prosecution didn't know was that when the murders occurred, I was outside of Puerto Rico, living in the state of Mississippi. After they found out, they alleged that I had the capacity to come to Puerto Rico, kill these people, and return to Mississippi, because, according to them, it wasn't a long distance. God's intervention prepared everything so that there would be no opportunity to doubt my innocence.

Without knowing when these murders occurred, I had been out looking for work. I was not Christian at the time, but in His ability to foresee the future, God had already set the stage for my good.

When I had gone to the job interview, I wanted them to give me the morning schedule because I didn't want the night shift at the restaurant. The manager gave me the job but told me the only shift available was the night shift. I wasn't too happy with the schedule, but I took it because I needed the job. What I didn't know was that the hand of

God was working in my favor because in the near future, a storm was headed my way in which I would be accused of murder and my life confined behind bars if found guilty.

Many times, we get upset when things don't turn out in our favor without knowing that God is aligning everything to prevent things in the future from harming us. We have to learn to completely trust in Him, even when we don't have all the details.

My lawyers proceeded to find the store manager in Mississippi, who was a White American, to present the information he had to prove my innocence. The day they presented the witness for the defense, he presented a pay stub and a punch card that showed the day and time when these murders occurred in Bayamón, Puerto Rico. God was so grand and powerful that the day these acts occurred was on the same day I had started work. That clearly proved I was innocent. I would have been serving several life sentences if God had not intervened. If I had worked a day later or with the morning shift that I wanted, I could have been found guilty because the prosecution would have shown that I could have come and gone and returned to Mississippi with plenty of time. God placed His powerful hand and ordered all things according to His purpose.

During the preliminary hearing, after both the prosecution and defense presented their cases, the judge would now decide my case. The courtroom was full, and the atmosphere was tense. When the time came for the judge to pronounce his sentence, he began to say that he wanted to make sure that when he retired, he was reassured he had not sent an innocent person to jail to serve a sentence, so he proceeded to say that he declared Raul Quiñones innocent of all charges against him, and the people in the court started to applaud and shout.

The inmates I was in jail with were following the case on the news, so they were able to hear what the judge had ruled. The judge gave orders for my immediate release, so they took me back to collect my things. When I arrived at the section where I was assigned, the inmates started to shout and applaud, and they said, "Christ did it! Christ did it!" Tears ran down my face.

When I arrived at my cell, I hugged my cellmate and said goodbye. As I was walking through the corridors, one of the inmates stopped me and told me that now he was in charge of preaching the Word of God.

God made the impossible possible and took into His hands the life of a child who began in a dysfunctional household as a juvenile delinquent and transformed him into an instrument to deliver a message of love, power, and transformation to the world for His glory and honor!

Juicio masacre 'Las Gardenias'

Tratan impugnar testimonio

Por Víctor González Orta
Redactor — EL VOCERO

● BAYAMON — Entrando ya en su etapa final el juicio contra 2 jóvenes acusados de 4 asesinatos por la llamada "Masacre de las Gardenias", ocurrida el 20 de febrero pasado, la Defensa ha sentado a declarar a jóvenes residentes de allí que han sido preguntados sobre cómo era el

Tratan...
(Viene de la Pág. 4)

joven de 14 años Joseph Guzmán Nieves, fue asesinado de varios disparos; y aunque él no pudo verlo por impedirlo la esquina de un edificio, también murió a balazos Luis R. Colón Capeles, "Papo". "Colin" dijo que vio a Solano Moreta apuntándole con un arma larga y disparándole, por lo que tuvo que correr buscando protección hacia un apartamento del segundo piso del Edificio 4 donde reside María Torres. Dijo que desde una ventana de ese apartamento vio al mismo acusado en una esquina del Edificio 6 apuntando con su arma larga a su hermano John, otro de los asesinados, quien cayó en medio de los edificios 4 y 6. "Colin" no dijo que Solano Moreta disparara contra su hermano, pero que sí lo hizo otro individuo, Raúl Quiñones quien era precedido por otro sujeto de apodo "Perlita".

Los letrados ponen en duda el testimonio del testigo debido a que se ha dicho que los alrededor de 15 sujetos que incursionaron en el residencial buscando a "Colin" por problemas personales vestían, según el testigo, ropas oscuras y algunos se cubrían con antifaces o chalecos con capuchas.

alumbrado la noche de los hechos, afirmando éstos en general que no existía o era pobre.

Entre estos testigos, las jóvenes Vicky y su hermana Sheila Carrasquillo Rodríguez y el joven Daniel "Danny" Jiménez, coincidieron en que tanto en la cancha como en otras áreas, el alumbrado era deficiente o no lo había. El punto es importante para los abogados del acusado Víctor Solano Moreta, Ledos. Ramón Delgado y Arturo Aponte Arche, así como para el Lcdo. Anthony Cuevas Ramos, abogado de Alfredo Figueroa Ayala "Papote".

La Defensa pretende impugnar a Leonel Berríos Torres, "Colin", quien es el testigo principal del fiscal Carlos J. Beltrán Meléndez. Ese testigo bajo inmunidad es el que ha alegado pudo ver como frente al Edificio 3 donde se encontraba su cuñado el

(Pasa a la Pág. 55)

Apela la extradición el soldado boricua detenido en Macedonia

Por CARMEN ENID ACEVEDO
DE EL NUEVO DIA

UN SOLDADO puertorriqueño destacado en Macedonia, ex república yugoslava, y a quien el Negociado Federal de Investigaciones (FBI) extradió a Filadelfia por cargos de asesinato relativos a una masacre ocurrida en Puerto Rico en febrero de 1993, apela la decisión de esa agencia de traerlo a la Isla para ser juzgado por los hechos.

Raúl Quiñones Echevarría de 26 años y quien residía en la Isla hasta el año pasado cuando se enlistó en las Fuerzas Armadas norteamericanas, sometió un recurso de apelación en Filadelfia, Pennsylvania, donde está ingresado en una prisión, tras ser extraditado de Macedonia el pasado 25 de agosto de este año.

Se espera que aunque Quiñones Echevarría está apelando la decisión de extradición para ser juzgado en el Tribunal Superior de Bayamón por los hechos de la Masacre de

Criminal (CIC) de Bayamón, circuló la información del acusado a través del FBI. Los agentes de la Policía Carlos Hornoto y Néstor López, rastrearon al

A su vez, los federales hicieron los contactos con la Interpol y la oficina del FBI en Bonn, Alemania, quienes dieron con el acusado.

EN LO QUE dejó perplejos a las autoridades estatales, Quiñones Echevarría fue detectado en Schweinsfurt, Alemania, donde se encontraba, pero rendía un servicio especial en Macedonia, y llegaron agentes federales a arrestarlo el pasado.

El hombre, quien se cree que había servido antes de reenlistar en 1993, está acusado de cuatro cargos de asesinato en primer grado y violación a la Ley de armas y tentativa de asesinato, en relación a la Masacre de las Gardenias, ocurrida en Bayamón el pasado primero.

Por esos hechos está cumpliendo cadena perpetua en la Cárcel de Las Cucharas en Ponce, Víctor Solano Moreta, de 27 años, hermano del notorio "Jorge "Wes" Moreta. También fueron acusados Juan "Perlita", quien todavía está prófugo y que se alega que es el lugarteniente de "Wes", Alfredo Rodríguez Ayala, conocido por "Chin" y Luis A. Aponte Figueroa, además

Se debilita...

(Viene de la Pág. 3)

tiene una hija procreada con Quiñones, sostuvo que el 20 de febrero del '95 mientras pasaba en carro acompañada por una amiga frente al Residencial Las Gardenias en Bayamón, se percató algo había pasado allí y tras enterarse de los asesinatos de 4 jóvenes, llamó a eso de las 11 P.M. a Misisipi para enterar a su novio de lo ocurrido en el residencial donde él tenía amigos y conocidos. La joven alegó que compañeros de cuarto de su novio le dijeron que él se encontraba trabajando en el turno de 4 P.M. a 12 de la medianoche y lo llamara después de esa hora. La joven lo volvió a llamar a la 1 A.M. del día 21 y le contó del incidente.

Fue después de esa declaración que el juez pidió a la defensa produjera para el 10 de enero del '95 al custodio de facturas de la Telefónica para que trajera la factura de la llamada hecha a Quiñones el día ya señalado. Pero el martes al llamarse el caso, la Telefónica informó no existía esa factura, por lo que la prueba de coartada de los abogados Ramón Delgado Rodríguez y Antonio Sagardía, quedó debilitada, aunque ellos sometieron al Tribunal copias de talonarios de cheques donde se hacía constar que su cliente trabajaba en el citado restaurant para la fecha de la masacre.

Sin embargo, el fiscal Carlos J. Beltrán Meléndez, en la vista del martes refiriéndose al cheque de febrero, trajo a colación que Quiñones recibía paga quincenal y había cobrado por sólo 17 horas de esa quincena que cubría del 8 al 21 de febrero. Quiñones así lo admitió y dijo que las 17 horas trabajadas fueron en los 2 últimos días de esa quincena pues había comenzado a trabajar en el restaurant ese día 20 recomendado por un compañero de cuarto. Quiñones también admitió que en todos los documentos suyos que ha presentado su Defensa ninguno tiene fecha de los días 20 ó 21 de febrero ni tampoco informan de los días específicos en que trabajó.

Quiñones, de 26 años, dijo al Fiscal que para febrero del '93 fue a residir con su cuñado Alberto Rivera a Gulfport, Misisipi y poco después se fue a vivir a un edificio de apartamentos. Admitió conocía a varias personas en Las Gardenias como el testigo estrella en el caso Leonel Berríos Torres "Colin" pero sólo en una actividad bailable; pero también conocía a Jorge "Wes" Solano Moreta, al hermano de éste Víctor, a otro involucrado conocido como "Perlita" y a "Chiri". Sobre Luis Agosto Figueroa "Chuco" no recuerda conocerlo. Reconoció que de los mencionados que eran miembros de la pandilla de "Wes", el único que tenía entrenamiento militar era el Quiñones, pues ha sido soldado desde abril del '89.

Quiñones dijo estuvo como un año fuera —del '92 al '93— de la Guardia Nacional de Puerto Rico y cuando se fue a Misisipi pidió el traslado a la Guardia Nacional de ese estado. Sostuvo vino a la Isla en noviembre del '93 y ese fue el único viaje que hizo y permaneció una semana aquí. Ese viaje dijo fue con el propósito de entregarse cuando se enteró por Sheila de que la Policía lo buscaba. El joven también admitió al Fiscal conocía a John Berríos (hermano de "Colin"), muerte directa con un rifle que se le atribuye por "Colin", y dijo John jugó baloncesto con él. A Quiñones además se le imputan los asesinatos del cuñado de "Colin", el joven de 14 años Joseph Guzmán Nieves, el de Luis Colón Capeles y el de Edwin Robles Carrión, y una tentativa de asesinato en "Colin".

El Lcdo. Sagardía en su informe final citó el que contra su cliente había un problema de identificación, pues "Colin" había dicho que el que disparó a su hermano era rubio y Quiñones no lo es. El Fiscal, por su parte, sostuvo que la defensa olvidó mencionar el resto de la descripción aceptada por el imputado, de que es tosco, que ha usado barba pegada, la edad aproximada y la estatura. Fue ahí que el juez decidió la defensa informara para el viernes si podía traer como testigo al dueño del Restaurant. Así la vista sigue el viernes 13 a las 9:00 A.M.

Minister in the Desert

As a member of the United States Armed Forces, I had the privilege of serving ten years as an infantryman and leader of a platoon of twenty-one soldiers. During my years serving in the Armed Forces, I had the privilege in 1994 to form part of a mission with the United Nations that was sent out to prevent a war between two different factions in Yugoslavia, in the province of Macedonia. I also formed part of the OTAN mission in 1995 to avoid a conflict between two factions in Bosnia.

Missions were very common for me as an infantryman, and we were always prepared to face conflicts around the world. Sometimes the missions had the goal of negotiating peace in the places assigned by the Army, and we also faced the possibility of conflict or war.

In 2003, we received a mission to go to Iraq because we had entered war with the president of that nation, Saddam Hussein. As soon as I found out and received the mission details of Iraq, I remembered a pastor that I had in the past who had told us that he had received orders to go to South Korea, and precisely when he was about to leave for the mission, he prayed, and God moved in a supernatural way where they stopped his journey to South Korea and changed his orders. He didn't have to go.

I began to think as a Christian that this was something that God could do in my case too, and when I received my orders for Iraq, I did exactly the same. I asked God to prevent me from going to Iraq for that conflict or war since, at the time, I was already a pastor at a local congregation and had a family with small children.

The last thing on my mind was that when we have our own agendas or plans on how we want to do things, God already has a perfect plan and purpose with everything He allows in our lives. God does not work by chance since God is omniscient, with the ability to know everything; omnipotent, with the ability to be all-powerful; and omnipresent, with the ability of being everywhere at the same time. He had a completely different plan than what I had asked Him.

The Word of God says in Jeremiah 33:3, "Ask me and I will tell you remarkable secrets you do not know about things to come." What this verse says is that every time we pray and call out to God, we know that He will answer us and that each prayer will have an answer from God in His time and in His way. That verse does not guarantee that God will answer us according to how we want, but He will reveal His purpose in terms of our request and His will for our lives.

Unlike the pastor who prayed, and God changed his orders, God allowed my mission to continue without delay. I kept seeing time pass by, and I did not see the answer how I wanted it, so I began to mentally prepare for my departure and prepare my heart to say goodbye to my family without knowing if I would ever return.

We were headed toward a battlefield and didn't know what the results would be. I didn't want to forget what the Word in Romans 8:28 states: "And we know that God causes everything to work together for the good of those who love God and are called according to his purpose for them."

When I arrived in Iraq after many hours of travel, I found myself in a desert where the temperature could reach 130° Fahrenheit, where you could sense the pain, need, suffering, and scarcity. I was entering a place completely unknown, and I was there to remove a dictator from his position because, according to our government, he had weapons of mass destruction to kill people en masse, and that was the mission that was given to us.

I didn't know how long I would remain at that place, and I was completely cut off from my family for the first few months, so they were unaware of my situation at this place. My family could watch the news that showed the critical situation of the war and talked about the number of deaths and casualties that occurred on a daily basis.

Can you imagine the families that had no communication with their loved ones because the war had begun, not knowing if one day they would receive the unfortunate news that their husband or the father of their children had died in combat?

We left on a mission without any guarantee of return. But God had a greater mission for Sergeant Raul Quiñones, who was in charge of twenty-one infantry soldiers during combat.

I found myself on various missions searching for the enemy in different places, and I experienced very sad things during those missions. I remember entering a house searching for the enemy or important members belonging to Saddam Hussein's army, and we had to kick down the doors to enter those houses with information we had received. Sometimes we didn't find the people we were looking for, but we did find mothers and small children crying and screaming because they thought we were going to eliminate everyone in that home. Those moments were difficult because every time I saw a woman crying and covering her children with her body like a hen keeps her chicks under her wings, it affected me emotionally to think that this woman could be a reflection of my wife and that her small children were just like my own whom I had left behind in the United States.

I found myself dealing with many missions of this nature. In others, our lives were in great danger as we were bombarded by the enemy, with missiles falling close to my soldiers and me without being able to protect them from the attacks.

My soldiers knew I was a Christian pastor, and they had different religions or beliefs. Being there made me reflect that sometimes we complain about places and circumstances in which we find ourselves without knowing that God has plans for us in that place and circumstance. Sometimes I'd question why God had allowed me to be away from my family and the church where I pastored, but God wanted to take me places I had never been to share the Word with others in critical situations. That is why when we pray to the Lord, we must always end it by asking that His perfect will be done in our plans and decisions because He can see the future and beyond what our natural eyes can see.

Some soldiers who were satanists and didn't believe in God would ask me to pray for them before we started the missions so that my angels, as they said, would protect them. How important it is to show our dependence on the Lord, even in the most critical moments of our lives! There will always be someone watching our behavior. They want to see if our trust is truly grounded in God. They will see that we have peace in the midst of the storm because our security is in the God we serve.

God gave me the privilege to speak with a Christian chaplain in the Army who was there so that we could create studies for the soldiers who wanted to listen to any type of spiritual advice. I took advantage of the opportunity because this captain was from South Korea and didn't speak English well since he had lived there all his life and only learned basic English. God opened a door of opportunity for me to connect with him and assist him with his chaplain duties.

I started giving Bible studies for the soldiers in the middle of a war and took advantage of the down time they gave us to gather the soldiers in a place where the enemy had stored ammunition that had been confiscated on previous missions. We cleaned up that space and began to give Bible studies, and the soldiers who heard the Word of God began to accept Jesus as Lord and Savior. It's impressive how human beings are more susceptible to listen to the Word of God and are more sensitive to the message God wants to bring to them during critical moments in their lives. Perhaps it is because of the fear of dying without having surrendered their lives to Jesus, but whatever the situation, they were ready to listen to the Word of God. I never imagined that part of my mission would be to start Bible studies for soldiers. That never crossed my mind since I went to Iraq for a war and fulfill my duties as a soldier.

I have come to the conclusion that man has his plans and then God imposes His without us even knowing it. For His glory, God uses the circumstances and situations in the lives of His children to make the best of it for us and others. Our hearts must be willing, available, and expectant for the mission that comes from above so that we can make an impact and difference to those around us. The Word of God teaches us that we are the light and salt of the earth and that the light cannot be hidden but must shine at all times (Matt. 5:13–16). Sometimes we as Christians tend to choose the places where we think we can share the Word instead of allowing the Holy Spirit to place us where we can touch lives with the message of salvation through the cross. You can be sure that God will open doors for you in places where doors were closed to others. God needs an army of willing, available, and voluntary people who have the love of Christ in their hearts to share the good news of the gospel without fear of rejection, ridicule, or adverse situations.

I thought my place to preach was during the service days in my congregation, but God allowed me to reach a place that I never imagined, a desert. Even in the desert, God can make you an instrument in His hands to carry a message while using that same place to shape your life as He uses you to continue to minister to others. The conditions to fulfill God's purpose and deliver the message of salvation won't always be perfect, but wherever God establishes you will always be a place of blessing. God will make the right conditions for you to go so that someone will hear the voice of God through your lips.

The soldiers began to receive Jesus as Lord and Savior, and it occurred to me to ask the chaplain, who was also a captain in the Army and who had connections in high places, if those soldiers who had surrendered their lives to Jesus could be baptized. Can you imagine what I was asking for in the middle of a war? The captain immediately reached out to his higher-ranking officials to see if the military engineers could make a hole in the desert in Iraq with their machinery. Surprisingly, the doors opened for the engineers to make a hole in a foreign land by means of a Christian soldier whom God was using in that place. I felt like an ambassador in distant lands delivering a message of salvation.

Finally, they made a fairly large hole, surrounded it with plastic, and filled it up with water. I had the blessing of baptizing the soldiers in the desert, something that was not on my agenda either but that God had as part of my résumé and relationship with Him. When we do things that we don't understand but do it in obedience to God, He will honor us, and His name will be glorified.

After several months had passed, I was able to communicate with my family and tell them that I was fine, but I had no information on when we would return to the United States since we had arrived when the war was starting and did not know how things would unfold.

That desert in Iraq was a place where God continued His work in me as a Christian, preacher, and ambassador of His kingdom. Our platoon did over one hundred missions in Iraq, where none of my soldiers, me included, were harmed by the enemy. God had not only protected me, but He also protected all those under my care as sergeant.

In another unexpected mission, I was placed in charge of enemies we had captured during missions from our platoon, and we kept them in custody in a place similar to a jail. We were assigned to watch over those captured soldiers who would be interrogated for their actions in combat. We had received classified information that they participated in attacks against our soldiers. We wanted to determine if they were truly guilty of those attacks against our soldiers or were simply innocent bystanders in the wrong place and time. Once again, I found myself in that place where I didn't know what God would do in the midst of this mission. As a Christian soldier, I wanted to be sure those captured were still treated as human beings while in the custody of me and my platoon.

On one occasion, I was going to give them water and apples given to us to feed them, but when I took the water bottles, I noticed they were hot due to the exposure of high temperatures in the desert. On the other hand, the apples were covered in dust because of the heavy winds. I was prepared to go to all of the cells and give them the hot water and dirty apples in the conditions they were in when I heard a voice inside me say: "Give them some of the cold water that you have, and clean the apples before you give it to them." The voice I heard didn't make any sense since these people were my enemies, and there was no need to treat them with courtesy, especially as a soldier. Keep in mind that to everyone's view, these people were our enemies who had been captured during combat after allegedly attacking our soldiers. However, the Word of God teaches us in Matthew 5:43–48:

> You have heard that it has been said, "You must love your neighbor and hate those who hate you." But I tell you, love those who hate you. Pray for those who do bad things to you and who make it hard for you. Then you may be the sons of your Father Who is in heaven. His sun shines on bad people and on good people. He sends rain on those who are right with God and on those who are not right with God. If you love those who love you, what reward can you expect from that? Do not even the tax-gatherers do that? If you say hello only to the people you like, are you doing any more than others? The people who do not know God do that much. You must be perfect as your Father in heaven is perfect.

These verses are easier to read than apply because that idea was against what I believed as a soldier, but I couldn't forget that I was a child of God first, put in a place to shine the light of Christ in me. We can't pretend to be Christians in one place and forget our identity when we are in another place where we think we can act differently.

Now I found myself in a position that the same person preaching to the soldiers and converting them to Christ had to apply the same principles in the Word of God to his enemies. Based on the voice that I heard, I obeyed, began to clean the apples, and went to get the cold water for these people. I didn't realize that those I was guarding were watching me as I went back and forth with this struggle with my humanity and God's desire to provide them with cold water and clean apples, but God, who is sovereign, was fulfilling His purpose in me and through me.

When I approached them to give them the water and apples, they were staring at me. One of them knew a little bit of English and asked for my name. I gave him my name, and he asked permission to ask me a question. After I said yes, he asked me why I cleaned the apples and gave them my cold water. He told me that they were watching me for a while and that my behavior toward them was different than other soldiers who guarded them during other hours of the day. That took me by surprise because I wasn't aware they had been watching me. They were amazed at my treatment toward them without knowing that I was initially at odds with God's orders, and finally decided to obey.

Sometimes as Christians we will disagree with God regarding something He asks of us, but in the end, the most important thing is to do what He asks, even if we don't fully understand what God is asking of us because that is what faith and obedience to God is all about.

Once they asked me that question, I quickly told them that the love of God in me that provoked me to display this act of compassion was the reason I cleaned the apples and gave them my cold water. This immediately opened the door to have a conversation about the God I was talking about. They were mostly Muslims, and their doctrine is completely different, although they have stories in their book called the Koran, where they mention characters in the Bible, like Abraham, Moses, and others.

In my mind, I immediately thought of giving theological or biblical explications of what I wanted to say, but it wouldn't make sense to them because they viewed Jesus as a prophet or messenger of God and not as the Son of God and Savior of the world. But again, I heard the voice of God telling me to preach Jesus through my acts of love toward them. God often requires us to preach from the Word that already exists in us, but we must preach by showing acts of love and compassion.

They continued observing my acts of compassion, love, and mercy, which caught their attention so much that they asked if I could sit with them in the cell to talk to them about my Christian beliefs. This could have been a dangerous act, but I felt peace and knew that everything would be alright.

At first, they would look at me and asked if I was Iraqi since our Latin features are very similar to theirs. In all these conversations, there was always one who spoke English with me, and he would translate the information to them in their language. I told them I was from Puerto Rico, and they had no idea where it was located on the map and began to compare it to Mexico. They knew about Mexico from the football games that are also played in Iraq.

The day came when I decided to step into the cell, and they sat in a circle and began to ask questions about my faith. It was impressive to see that they accepted me as one of their own, but I knew it was the hand of God giving me the opportunity to show His love through me.

I remember one day when one of them told me that my face shined inexplicably. I knew it was the light of Christ through His children to make a difference in a dark world where we see continuous pain and suffering. The Word of God says: "You are the light of the world. You cannot hide a city that is on a mountain. Men do not light a lamp and put it under a basket. They put it on a table, so it gives light to all in the house. Let your light shine in front of men. Then they will see the good things you do and will honor your Father Who is in heaven" (Matt. 5:14–16). The day I decided to step inside the cell with them, I told a fellow soldier to hold my rifle and close the cell behind me. Once I stepped in, they said to me a word in Iraqi that meant welcome to the circle of friends. I felt in total control and shared what Jesus meant to me, and they listened attentively, which was a very special moment.

They remained in that jail for some time as the United States Army investigated who they were, if they were part of Saddam Hussein's army, the president of Iraq, or if they were involved in the attacks on American soldiers. After the investigation was complete, it turned out that there was not enough evidence against many of them, so they were set free.

The day they were set free, I was working my shift and remember that while they were opening the cell doors, something took me by surprise. Before they left the place, they lined up in front of me to hug me and give me three kisses on the cheek, which is customary in countries in the Middle East. While each of them did this, they started to walk out, shouting, "Raul, we love you, and if you want to visit us, we will protect you." One of them took off a silver ring and gave it to me as a gift and to remember them by.

I cannot guarantee that they accepted Jesus as Lord and Savior, but I do know that God touched their hearts and allowed them to meet a person who showed them the love of Christ even though we were in a combat zone. We know that what God begins, He finishes in a glorious way.

You can only imagine the mixed emotions I feel when I look back at these two stages in my life and the lessons that came with them. I am the tangible evidence of God's faithfulness and covering, from preserving my life in Puerto Rico, deflecting bullets that were fired at me to kill me; His grace throughout the judicial process, where a 305-year life sentence was overruled, and I was able to embrace freedom again; and now seeing this man accused of a massacre become part of the United States Armed Forces and in a war zone, preaching the gospel, adding souls to the kingdom of God, baptizing them in the middle of the desert, and having the opportunity to love and minister to our enemies. It has all been through grace and mercy for His glory! My whole life is a testimony, but if you thought that I had faced death only on those two occasions, you are wrong. I still have to share another event where I danced with death.

Raúl Quiñones
J.R.
your brother

GRADUATION

Another Dance with Death

In our fragile humanity, we find ourselves frequently having so many questions in the midst of difficult circumstances in life, and we often don't understand how, when, or why God does things the way He does. As Christians, we can't possibly fit God into a mold or equation where we think that how He dealt with someone in their crisis is how He will deal with the next person. God is sovereign and knows that each person and their process is different. He works with them like a potter who is able to see the final product from the moment He starts working. He shapes our lives to make us more like His Son Jesus but does it by working with each person in distinct ways just like we see in the Bible and what He did with two blind men.

In this story, we see Jesus healing a blind man as follows: "After Jesus had said this, He spit on the ground. He mixed it with dust and put that mud on the eyes of the blind man. Then Jesus said to him, 'Go and wash in the pool of Siloam.' The man went away and washed. When he came back, he could see" (John 9:6–7). We then see Jesus healing another blind man with another method: "Then Jesus put His hands on their eyes and said, 'You will have what you want because you have faith.' Their eyes were opened. Jesus told them to tell no one" (Matt. 9:29–30). They both had the same condition of blindness, but He used different methods to deal with their faith in Him.

The methods Jesus used were different in some cases, but the end result was the same. Jesus wanted people to recognize the power He carried as a sign that He was the promised Messiah and the Son of God. "But if I do them, even if you do not believe Me, believe the works that I do. Then you will know the Father is in Me and I am in Him" (John 10:38). It was His desire that human beings understand that faith placed in Him produces changes in their lives, both physically and spiritually.

No human being wants to go through adversity, crisis, or conflicts, but these are what God sometimes uses to give us spiritual formation so that we can have a personal experience with Him that, otherwise, we would not have valued. This book, as you have read so far, is a compilation of personal experiences under different circumstances in which God worked in various ways in areas in my life that needed to be transformed, healed, or changed.

Although at the beginning of my crisis, I had doubt, pain, and fear, at the end of my painful experience, I was able to see the other side of the coin and confirm that I had grown and matured in many areas of my life and in my relationship with God.

These events were written to motivate readers to think that there still is and always will be the hope that God will do something miraculous in our difficult circumstances, but we have to put our trust and faith in Him and give Him the opportunity for His process to work in our lives as only He knows how. I don't intend to convince you through this book that I know everything about how God works in every circumstance but that these pages simply have real-life events where God operated miraculously in my life from the inside out. I must emphasize that He didn't always answer my prayers the way I wanted, but He always answered them according to His plan, His purpose, and in His time.

In March 2020, something unexpected occurred that wasn't part of my plan or was included in my prayers. I never I would be infected with a virus so lethal that would put me between life and death. The coronavirus was spreading at a rapid pace around the world, causing devastation.

In the Bible we find Jesus speaking: "I have told you these things so you may have peace in Me. In the world you will have much trouble. But take hope! I have power over the world!" (John 16:33). I have mentioned this verse many times in different sermons, but it was this event that caused me to understand it more personally and clearly. Sometimes the Word of God becomes easier to understand, and we manage to trust it more through the difficult events that occur in our lives and where our experience with pain helps us see things like a mirror reflecting God's message and intentions.

Jesus never said in His Word that I could overcome any affliction in this world, but He said that He had overcome all the ways in which affliction could manifest itself over our lives and, therefore, as His Holy Spirit dwells in us, we would receive the ability to endure and walk through it victoriously. God won't aways take us out of the fiery furnace of a trial, but we will have His company through any hardships we face. He will take the helm of the boat of our lives, and despite the strong storms and winds of our crises, we can be sure that He will end up in a safe harbor because He is our guide. "For the Lord will not turn away from His people. He will not leave His chosen nation" (Ps. 94:14).

If you ask any Christian, he or she will most likely tell you that he or she does not wish to go through any problems, crises, tribulations, or tests. The Word of God records people like the apostle Paul, Jesus's disciples, and Joseph, among others, who arrived at their purpose through many difficult circumstances,. Those trials were what made them grow in their faith and brought them closer to God. "In each city they helped the Christians to be strong and true to the faith. They told them, "We must suffer many hard things to get into the holy nation of God" (Acts 14:22).

On March 24, 2020, I returned home in the afternoon after being at work with a headache that I had never felt or experienced before. The pain began while at work, but I didn't want to leave my work unfinished; instead, I wanted to complete it and then go back home so I could rest or take a pill strong enough to control the unbearable headache.

When I arrived home, I couldn't stand the pain, and I had to tell my wife to take me to the doctor. When I arrived at the hospital, I was running a low-grade fever, but since the hospitals at that time were at capacity due to the pandemic, they evaluated me and told me that if the fever spiked, to return, so, they sent me back home.

The coronavirus pandemic had spread throughout the United States, and they were trying to manage the overcrowding of patients who had been admitted to the hospitals. They were dealing with different conditions they still did not have answers to resolve the problem of knowing how the coronavirus manifested in patients and what kind of medicines they could give to handle the different reactions they were having.

In the midst of all this, I found myself part of the chaos that existed, both for the doctors and for the sick patients who could not receive the appropriate treatment because they did not know how this virus manifested in people. I was tested to see if I had the virus, and after ten days, the results came back negative. What was interesting was that I was experiencing all the symptoms the doctors were saying this virus carried; however, the test they gave me came back negative, which was another problem within the medical system. The tests used to determine if a patient had the virus were deficient and did not always give the correct results, according to what some doctors told me. The problem at that time was that those tests weren't dependable, often giving results contrary to the symptoms. This provoked an even bigger crisis for the doctors.

With the negative test result, the doctors began to treat my condition as if I had the flu virus, which was the best they could do for me at the time. The problem was that the medicines were not working for me. I had to go to the doctor a second time, and they did another test that came back negative, and this was baffling the doctors who were treating me.

They saw all the coronavirus symptoms, but the results kept coming back negative.

They sent me back home, but I physically worsened. It got so bad that I dropped approximately fifteen to twenty pounds in one week. I lost my ability to taste and smell, had body aches, completely lost my appetite, had a fever, couldn't breathe properly, and couldn't walk or stand on my own. Little by little, I felt my life draining away.

My wife decided to wear masks and gloves to protect herself because even though the tests were negative, all the symptoms showed I had the virus, and she wanted to take the necessary precautions. My wife was my caretaker, and she witnessed how I began to deteriorate day after day without finding a solution. We had to make the decision to tell my children who still lived at home to stay at the house of my other daughter who was already married to prevent them from getting infected. My wife and I treated those symptoms as if I had the coronavirus, and we did not want to take any chances.

These were times of intense mental, emotional, and physical battles s I cried out to God to give me a chance to live. I felt closer to the verge of death, and at that time, none of my material possessions were of any importance to me. I only thought about my family and how I didn't want to leave them alone.

Sometimes people wait for life-and-death moments to realize and evaluate what truly matters. The material things we possess will not accompany us on our journey toward death. But the experiences, quality time, love, and our testimony of how we serve the Lord will be what remain in the hearts and minds of our loved ones.

It was a spiritual battle in which Satan was trying to place doubt in every sermon that I had previously preached and heard, all the messages I had prepared, and every scripture I had read. Every piece of information I had of the Bible was being put to the test in that moment of pain, fear, and sadness.

Many times at night when while sleeping on the living room couch, tears ran down my cheeks while I wondered when this would end and how my life had unexpectedly changed from one moment to another. The time had come when my faith was being tested after preaching and serving the Lord for several years. It was as if a spiritual exam had been given to me to assess my relationship with God.

Many times we think that tomorrow is promised, and we make short and long-term plans, believing that it will all turn out as we have planned it. The truth is that planning is a very responsible concept, but making sure it will happen is to assume something that we don't know, and only God fully does.

I began to remember Job's story in the Bible (Job 1), a godly man who walked with the Lord in obedience and fear, who had many riches, possessions, and a beautiful family, but he would face the most painful moment of his life. Job was unaware that a conversation between God and Satan was taking place, and he would be the person God would use to show Satan that there was a person who had never seen Him face to face yet would never betray or be disloyal to Him as Satan, who had seen God face to face and betrayed that relationship.

I would never compare my situation to Job's, but I did feel alone when, in reality, God was always there with me. Moments of crisis, problems, and conflicts are those in which we wonder if God is with us or not, but it also allows us to see if our faith is real or not. It makes me think of another story in the book of Mark (4:35–41), where Jesus, after having fed thousands of people, told His disciples to prepare to cross over to the other side. The last thing they imagined was that a storm would break out in the midst of the calm waters in which they found themselves. Jesus was sleeping in the stern of the boat when the strong winds suddenly began to blow and the tides began to rise, so much so that the disciples feared for their lives, forgetting the words Jesus had told them about crossing to the other side.

God will always give us words of reassurance in times of peace so that in times of crisis, we are ready to remember the Word He spoke to us. Jesus said, "I have told you these things so you may have peace in Me. In the world you will have much trouble. But take hope! I have power over the world!" (John 16:33). God never promised us that in our relationship with Him, everything would fine and dandy, that we would have abundance, or that there wouldn't be problems until His second coming. On the contrary, He warned us about the hardships we would face in life. He also reaffirmed that we wouldn't be alone through those moments of crisis, fear, and uncertainty.

The disciples on the boat were trying to resolve the issue by their own strength, trying to take out the water without achieving their goal; the tides and strong winds pushed even more water into the boat than they could take out. At the end of their struggle to resolve the situation, they had forgotten that Jesus was in the boat, and they had already witnessed Him do many supernatural things. They had witnessed Jesus provide food for thousands of people, and counting on Him in the midst of their crisis was their best option.

Many times, difficult moments make us forget not only the words that God tells us about trusting Him but also try to resolve our conflicts through our own efforts when we know in advance that we cannot. We realize that the problem is bigger than us but forget that it will never be bigger than God.

When they saw their efforts were in vain, they decided to wake Jesus, not because they knew He could solve the problem, but as a final option of criticism and confrontation by letting Him know of a problem He knew beforehand and had a solution for.

Crisis will add such heavy burdens that we often forget that God is aware of our problems beforehand and always provides a solution. Desperation distracts us, and we put all our energy and effort into the problem instead of placing all our faith in the one who has our solution. It's our fallen nature and pride that makes us think we can solve any problem without God. Many times, God allows circumstances into our lives to show our weakness and need to call on Him and make Him part of not only our problems but our lives as well.

The disciples were about to be surprised to see how Jesus was going to solve a situation that was impossible for them. This miracle Jesus was about to perform was another sign for them to prove that He was the person He said He was. God's intervention in our problems and crises often reaffirms our faith in the things we have read in His Word and proves that it's true.

When they tried to wake Jesus from His sleep, they were resorting to their last solution to a situation that was out of their hands, and Jesus heard the disciples' screams and worry. He got up and confronted what was causing them fear. Immediately He rebuked the winds and waves, and everything became calm. The disciples, seeing what had happened, were perplexed to see how Jesus, with a few simple but powerful words, had calmed the storm that appeared in their lives. They forgot the words of Jesus when He said, "Let's go to the other side."

When we forget God's words, it's easy to fall into desperation, worry, and fear in the face of the circumstances before us. In the book of Hebrews 11:1, it says: "Faith shows the reality of what we hope for; it is the evidence of things we cannot see." We are required to have assurance and trust that what God spoke for us, despite the circumstances changing around us, the Word of God remains firm before any adversity that presents itself in our lives. It's easy to trust God when things are good, but it requires a mature faith when things dramatically turn for the worse.

People don't want things to change around them because we are creatures of habit, and when something changes outside of what we know as normal in our lives, it immediately brings anxiety and worry. We must understand that we must hold on and believe the Word of God despite the circumstances that can cause discomfort and change our plans. That is why faith is necessary when God allows something unexpected to change our plans and schedules.

The disciples were shocked by what they were witnessing before their eyes, and they began to talk among each other, saying, "Who is this, that even the winds and waves obey Him?" At that moment, they realized they didn't know Jesus as they thought they did. Jesus was not surprised by the storm because He knows all things, and that is why He rested and was confident in His mission that the Father had assigned Him was not yet complete. Therefore, He knew He wouldn't drown because it was clear to Him that He would die on a cross for humanity's sins. This is why, as children of God, we must be clear that God has control over our lives and that nothing and no one can change what God has established from eternity. We feel secure in knowing that God is in control of our lives and that whatever happens is because He allows it, even if we don't understand everything at the time.

Faith takes us to a place of acceptance, that no matter what happens, God's final product cannot be altered it without His consent. It is easier to rest in peace knowing these principles and trusting that God has the best desire and plan for our lives. Pain and suffering can make you criticize, doubt, curse, or accuse God of your circumstances, crises, or problems. At the same time, pain can also bring out your greatest and strongest worship. "I called to the Lord in my trouble. I cried to God for help. He heard my voice from His holy house. My cry for help came into His ears" (Ps. 18:6).

We must always choose to worship God, even if we don't have all the details or answers to what we are going through. We need to ask ourselves, "Do I want to guide my pain, words, and frustrations toward God in a negative way? Or do I want to cast my burdens to God in the form of trust and faith? We know He never fails, that He never forsakes us and won't ever leave us because His presence is in us and with us.

God is not intimidated by our worst moment because what seems to destroy us, many times is the process He uses to build in us character, dependency, and increase our faith. The story in Mark 4:35–41 ends with Jesus rebuking the winds and waves and His disciples surprised to see how he brought great peace. They marveled at how creation was subjected to Him by a word that He spoke. In their shame, they were only expressed to Jesus stay away from them because they were sinners. It wasn't Jesus's desire to stay away from them but to teach them to depend and trust the one who had called them to follow Him. Even though they were sinners, His mission was to die for all of humanity's sins. They found themselves at a loss for words amid their distrust toward Him.

After seeing the hand of God work in our lives, many times, we feel overwhelmed by the ignorance and fragility that we possess when we do not acknowledge His supernatural power to solve any circumstance. They felt unworthy of His grace, which, like them, was given to us not because we deserved it but because we received it in faith.

As my pain intensified from the coronavirus symptoms, I felt my faith being battered by the winds and tides of life. I had recently finished a three-day preaching campaign in which I had seen God's victory and His powerful work in many lives. The last thing on my mind was that I would face something that would put my life on the brink of death a few days later.

After several trips to the hospital, I could no longer bear the pain, and we returned to the hospital once more. I remember I told God in prayer to please not let me die, and I immediately began to cry, but a question from God came to my mind and heart. I felt God telling me, "You tell me not to let you die, and I ask you, why do you want to live?" It was a shocking question because when I asked God not to let me die, I was thinking of my family, children, and grandchildren.

People usually want to live to achieve their own successes and dreams, but we do not stop to think about why God gave us life and why we live. There are people who live simply to accumulate wealth and material things, and others who simply do not want to live because they have gone through difficulties in their lives and cannot find a reason to live.

In my case, He was refocusing me on the priorities in my relationship with Him. I couldn't forget that God had rescued me from a very dark world of evil and sin, and He wanted me to focus on the call He had given me. It wasn't that God didn't care about my family but He simply wanted me to place Him first as a child of God who was redeemed and bought at the price of blood. God didn't want me to forget His plan, purpose, and calling in my life. Situations arise when people are blessed by God, and then they forget about Him and focus on the blessings instead of on the Giver of the blessings.

The Word of God says, "First of all, look for the holy nation of God. Be right with Him. All these other things will be given to you also" (Matt. 6:33). In that verse, we can find God's priorities and desire to bless our lives and that nothing and no one will occupy the first place that only belongs to Him.

I remember the days passed, and I kept getting worse. My birthday was approaching, and the furthest from my mind was that I would not be able to celebrate that special day with my family since my children were in my other daughter's house, and my wife was the only one left with me in the house.

On my birthday, my wife told me to go and look out of the living room window, and when I looked, I saw my children with my grandson in the front yard. They were carrying a birthday cake with a candle and began to sing happy birthday from a distance since we were divided by the house window. It was very cold that day, but my family was willing to continue to support me in the midst of my pain from the virus, even if it was just looking at me through the outside window of the living room. When I saw them, my heart shattered, and I was in tears, and all I could do was place my hand up against the window while they did the same on the other side because I did not want them to enter the house for fear of getting infected with what I had. It was a moment of many tears on both sides, but I could hear them through the window singing the birthday song to me. Even my small grandson put his hand on the window, and I put mine on the other side of the window because it was the closest I could be to him.

After so many days of pain, I had no choice but to go to the emergency room to see what they could do for me. I could barely walk, and they had to look for a wheelchair to take me into the emergency room. When the doctor saw me, he asked two nurses to help me walk to see how far I could walk without help, but I had the nurses by my side just in case they had to hold me to not fall. When I started taking several steps, I couldn't go any further and was lacking oxygen, so they had to give me morphine intravenously to deal with the pain. Then the doctor proceeded to take some X-rays to see the conditions of my lungs. When the results came in, he came straight to my room and told me that in the thirty years that he had been working, he had never seen lungs so stained and destroyed like mine were. I didn't expect to hear those words, and it broke my heart when he said there was nothing that he could do for me. That was the moment when God reminded me that all men have limits in what they can do and that only God can operate in the impossible.

The doctor decided to call an ambulance and take me to a larger hospital because he didn't know how to deal with my situation. God in His Word advises us and warns us to put our total trust in man because they have limitations in what they can achieve, even in medicine. Psalm 146:3 says, "Put not your trust in princes, nor in the son of man, in whom there is no help."

An ambulance came to pick me up at the emergency clinic to take me to the other hospital and was taken to the intensive care unit of the hospital due to the condition I was in. I had never seen myself in critical condition. There are storms that come into our lives that take us by surprise and often make us wonder if we will be able to overcome them. This is when we have to embrace the Word and not allow our emotions to get the best of us. The Scriptures say (Ps. 23:4), "Yes, even if I walk through the valley of the shadow of death, I will not be afraid of anything, because You are with me. You have a walking stick with which to guide and one with which to help. These comfort me." This verse does not tell us that God will deliver us from our problems, but there is a promise that He will be with us through any circumstance. His company is more than enough in any crisis or adversity that we can face.

Something impressive happened while I was admitted in the hospital. As soon as I arrived, I felt a peace I couldn't explain. It was like an assurance that everything was would be okay because God was with me during my critical health. "The peace of God is much greater than the human mind can understand. This peace will keep your hearts and minds through Christ Jesus" (Phil. 4:7).

From a human perspective, the medical evidence pointed out that I was in a delicate situation, but from God's point of view, my condition was something He could resolve.

It's exactly the behavior of human frailty that evaluates things from an earthly perspective that will always show signs that your situation is in critical condition and that perhaps there is no solution ahead. It is so hard to believe in a critical situation humanly speaking while at the same time be willing to trust that my situation is not the end until God says the last word. Proverbs 16:9 says, "The mind of a man plans his way, but the Lord shows him what to do."

I didn't expect to end up in the intensive care unit. Nor did I imagine that what would become intense in that room was the demand that God would give me in the midst of my pain and suffering. When I got there, they immediately gave me oxygen to facilitate my breathing along with medication to relieve my pain. In addition to everything I was experiencing from the coronavirus and the deterioration of my lungs. I also developed a blood clot between my lung and heart. Immediately the following day, the doctors began investigating how I had a pulmonary embolism.

Every morning the nurses came in to take blood and give me blood thinners used with the intention to prevent present and future clots. There were always new nurses and doctors every time they came to speak with me and do the evaluations. They started evaluating my legs and stomach with an ultrasound machine to see if the blood clots started in my legs or if I had a family history to explain the condition, but I didn't have any, and I didn't have any family members who suffered from this condition. There were no blood clots in my legs, which took them by surprise since they normally start in the legs and then move to other parts of the body.

In the three days I was there, they continued searching and seeking answers on how to proceed with my condition. I was in a lot of pain during this time, couldn't breathe on my own, and had lost my appetite. However, I continued to feel that inexplicable peace within me, telling me, "No matter the tests or studies they do to you or how you feel, I (God) have complete control over your situation.

On one of the nights in the hospital without being able to receive visits due to the high risk of coronavirus exposure, which was at its highest peak at the time, I felt I had the greatest presence than any other human could have, and that was the company of the Sovereign God Almighty. On one of those nights that I was about to fall asleep, I heard the voice of God tell me: "Go to social media and start o preaching and worshiping me in the midst of your circumstance." Sometimes God will ask us to do things we typically do when things are good, but He will ask during the most difficult moments of your life because that is exactly what will forms character in us and prevents us from worshiping only when things are good.

God told me to do a Facebook live and preach and worship in the middle of my pain. One night I opened my personal page and started speaking the words that God was placing in my heart, and I tried to sing hymns of worship, but the pain was unbearable. I had to pause continuously between the message and worship for lack of air. At the same time, it was a privilege and an immense joy to worship God and speak of His wonders in the midst of my storm.

The song I began to sing spoke of His fidelity. This brought to mind the situation in which Paul and Silas found themselves after having been beaten many times and put in jail simply for casting out a spirit of divination in a young girl from whom her masters had profited. In the midst of their pain from the beatings and of being falsely placed in jail, instead of lamenting and complaining, they decided to worship the Lord with prayer and songs of praise. Acts 16:25 says, "About midnight Paul and Silas were praying and singing songs of thanks to God. The other men in prison were listening to them."

I realized the following day after having preached and worshiped God through social media, more than 63,000 people had viewed the message on Facebook. God used my condition to bring a message of salvation and reconciliation.

Let me briefly summarize this story that led me to face death again and see the hand of God bring me back to life. I never thought a virus like this would affect me in such a way, where my physical body deteriorated to such a degree that the same pastor that ran through stands and countries preaching in crusades for hours could no longer walk in a straight line or ten steps.

I developed several conditions caused by the virus, including a pulmonary embolism. My family delivered me into the hands of doctors without knowing if I'd leave the hospital again.

My finances were affected, but to this day we are seeing God's covering and how He touched the heart of many people to cover our basic needs. I saw how many people stood in the gap to fight and pray for my life when neither my family nor I had the strength to do so, as I also saw others remain silent.

I lived far from my wife, kids, grandchildren, congregation, and even all the pastoral ministries in which I was motivated with great fear of not being able to preach again. My family suffered a lot, and when I was at my weakest point, God told me, "Connect and preach." That livestream video is still being viewed by many people. I danced once again with death, but once again, God breathed life into me.

Today, God continues motivating me and giving me the grace and power to continue preaching His Word despite still recovering from the side effects of the coronavirus. We won't always have the perfect conditions to serve God, but God wants us to continue trusting Him the same way the apostle Paul expressed it in 2 Corinthians 12:10: "I receive joy when I am weak. I receive joy when people talk against me and make it hard for me and try to hurt me and make trouble for me. I receive joy when all these things come to me because of Christ. For when I am weak, then I am strong."

They told me I have permanent damage to my lungs based on the doctor's final diagnosis, but the experience I lived on the verge of death taught me to trust God more and value my family more, manage time correctly, and invest it in those things that truly matter, to serve Him with greater passion, enjoy life without rush, and be willing and available for whatever God asks of me. I learned that time does not discriminate, does not go back, does not stagnate, but always moves forward. I came to the conclusion that there is no time to waste time.

ARMY

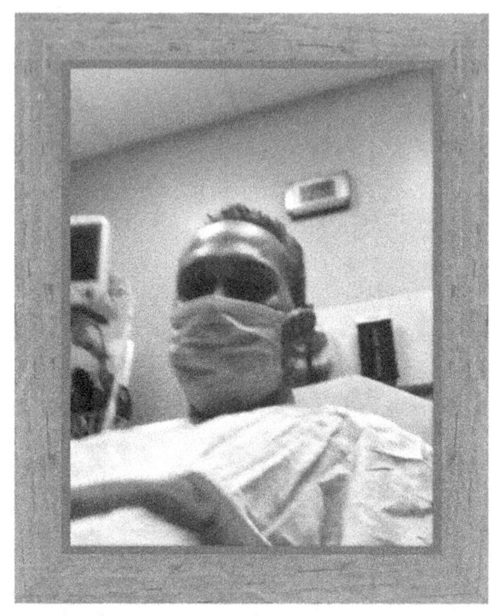

From My Pastoral Heart

I hope that this book has touched the most intimate parts of your heart and that through the testimonies within it, you were able to grasp a small picture or perspective of the greatness of God's power, see how much He loves His creation, and His desire to have an intimate relationship with people. It's his desire to give you purpose and eternal life, which this world can't offer.

The Word of God says in John 3:16–17, "For God so loved the world that He gave His only Son. Whoever puts his trust in God's Son will not be lost but will have life that lasts forever. For God did not send His Son into the world to say it is guilty. He sent His Son so the world might be saved from the punishment of sin by Him." Jesus, who was righteous, died for us, the unrighteous; being sinless, He died for us, sinners. He became a curse on the cross so that we would receive the blessing of salvation and eternal life. He became a man to die on a cross for us so that we could be blessed and seated in heavenly places with Christ Jesus.

Only Jesus could reconcile us with God by taking humanity's sins upon Himself by dying on the cross of Calvary, and He did so out of love for you and me. If you wish to accept Jesus as your Lord and Savior, repeat this prayer with me: "Lord Jesus, I accept you as Lord and Savior, and in faith and repentance, I believe what you did on the cross for me. Thank you for giving me a new life, and I ask this in the name of Jesus, amen."

If you made this prayer, you have become a child of God, saved by His grace and His love. I encourage you to look for a church where you can gather so that together with brothers and sisters in the faith who have also accepted Christ, you can continue to learn the Word of God, which will lead you to an intimate relationship with Him, where you will have experiences with Him and find your purpose in this life and then in eternal life with Jesus. May God bless you greatly!

-Pastor Raul Quiñones

I love my family ♡

OUR HAPPY PLACE

About the Author

Pastor Raul Quiñones was born on April 3, 1968, in Brooklyn, New York, and was raised in the city of Bayamón, Puerto Rico. His father, Raul Quiñones, died when he was young, and his mother, Abad Echevarría, raised him. He is one of four children: Awilda Román, Heriberto Román, and Louis Raúl Quiñones.

Raul has had a beautiful marriage for twenty-seven years at the closing of this book with his wife Sheila Marie Quiñones, with whom he has four children: Alieshka Marie Quiñones, Rashelle Rivera, Shylane Quiñones, and Louis Hiram Quiñones. He also has the blessing of having three grandchildren: Caleb Noe Rivera, Josías Yael Rivera, and Josué Eli Quiñones.

With a bachelor's degree in pastoral ministries from Nazarene Bible College in Colorado, he has been pastoring the Centro Mundial de Alabanza Church in Colorado Springs, Colorado, for fifteen years. God has given him the privilege of preaching in different places, such as the United States, Panama, Puerto Rico, Colombia, Costa Rica, Mexico, and Iraq, among others. He is also blessed to be part of the Alianza Ministerial de Colorado Springs Hispanic committee and the COSILoveYou American alliance of Colorado Springs, where he has served the needs of his city of Colorado Springs. His greatest goals are to preach the gospel so that souls come to know Christ, the lost be reconciled, to give his family and those who have surrounded him with a real testimony of his words and deeds of how important God is in the life of the human being, what God has done in him and through him for His glory and honor, and trying to be the best husband, father, grandfather, neighbor, citizen, human, son, brother, brother in Christ, and servant of God that he could be.

www.ingramcontent.com/pod-product-compliance
Lightning Source LLC
Chambersburg PA
CBHW071327130726
47996CB00002B/653